Plants Grow
Almost Anywhere

CONCEPT SCIENCE

Written by Colin Walker . Illustrated by Sally Simons

D1358628

Plants grow almost anywhere . . .

on deserts

in soil

n mountains

in lakes and rivers

and in the sea.

We can find plants growing . . .

in the soil

on top of water

in salt water

and in fresh water.

Plants are found all over the world.

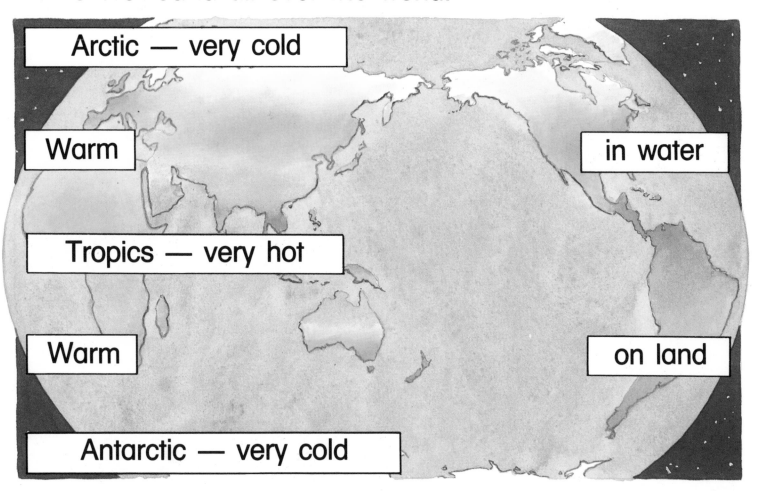

Arctic — very cold

Warm

in water

Tropics — very hot

Warm

on land

Antarctic — very cold

Plants can grow in very unusual places. . .

on poles

on other plants

on posts

under leaves

under stones

. . . even in or on us!

Some plants live in special places.
A crocus grows in cold places.

Cactus plants live in the desert.
It may be very hot during the day and
very cold at night.

Palms live in the tropics.
It is often very hot and
very wet in the tropics.

Mangroves live in salty water
and soil.

Water-lilies live in fresh water.

Mosses and ferns live in damp places.

Seaweeds live in the sea.

Banana trees
live in sunny places.

Many plants have special parts
that help them to live
in special places.

Most cactus plants store water
in their thick stems.
It does not rain often
in the desert.

Floating plants often have
tiny roots.
Their flat leaves float
on the surface
of the water.

Some plants have
hairy or furry leaves.
These plants do not
dry out easily.

Some plants have prickles —
Some animals do not eat these plants.

Wherever plants grow they almost always need . . .

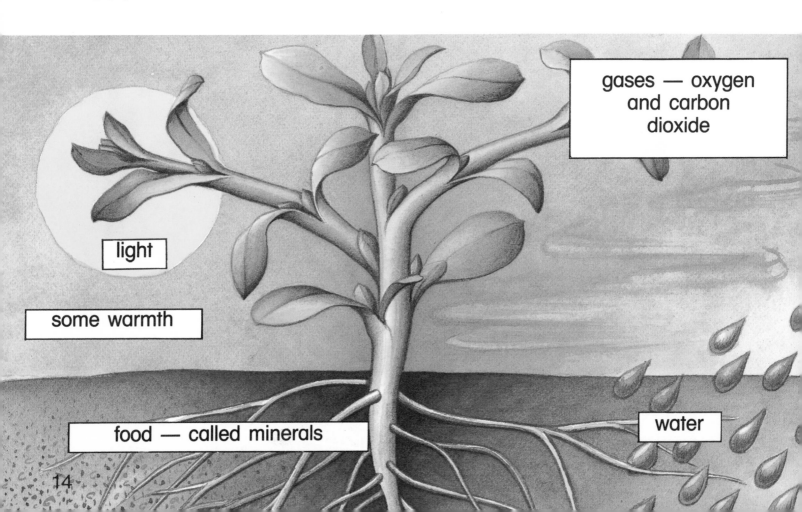

gases — oxygen and carbon dioxide

light

some warmth

food — called minerals

water

QUIZ

Ask your friend these questions . . .

Where do these plants grow?

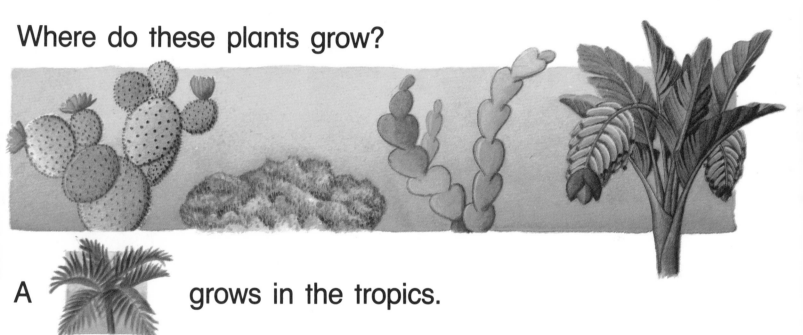

A  grows in the tropics.

A grows in damp places.

What does the  store inside itself?

Why don't  get eaten by most animals?

Name two things that plants get from the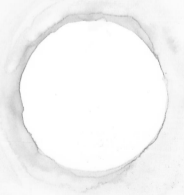